www.finishinglinepress.com

Bright Holes in the Dark

poems by

Beverly Mach Geller

Finishing Line Press
Georgetown, Kentucky

Bright Holes in the Dark

ACKNOWLEDGMENTS

Acknowledgment is made with thanks to the publications in which the following
poems first appeared, some in different forms or with different titles.

Derondareview.org: "Shabbat in Jerusalem"
Jewish Women's Literary Annual: "Late Autumn: Traveling the Roads of My
Childhood"
Kelsey Review: "Cataract Surgery," "Daughter," "Valentine (Memo for My
Husband)," "My Friend the Artist Gregorio Prestopino Addresses His Portrait of
His Mother, *Standing Woman*," "Remembering My Friend Nane"
NJ Poetry Society: "Sixties Reprise for Cousin Harry"
U.S.I Summer Fiction: "Bump and Butt of Passing Years," "Primavera Everlasting"

My thanks to: members of the Twin Rivers Writers' Group, Nancy Demme, Don
Lasko, Lois Marie Harrod, Janice Kaplan, Leah Maines, Christen Kincaid, my
husband Sam.

Very special thanks to: Lavinia Kumar, Antonia Sullivan, Carolina Morales.

Publisher: Leah Maines

Editor: Christen Kincaid

Cover Art: Rudall30/Shutterstock

Author Photo: Sam Geller

Cover Design: Elizabeth Maines

Printed in the USA on acid-free paper.
Order online: www.finishinglinepress.com
        also available on amazon.com

Author inquiries and mail orders:
Finishing Line Press
P. O. Box 1626
Georgetown, Kentucky 40324
U. S. A.

Table of Contents

For my husband, children, grandchildren, great grandchildren
who bring the brightness

Journey

As I make my way
down life's brambled path
thorns tear my skin

Measure of Days

Autumn winds bluster
a lone leaf clings to the plum tree
defying winter

Toward the Edge

Day night day night day
I catch the last rays of sun—
time's wheels are whirling

Late Autumn: Travelling the Roads of My Childhood

Goldenrod and Queen Anne's lace
once grew here
I don't see milkweed either
we blew milkweed silk
it rode on the wind
corn stalks are turning brown
cabbage is rotting in the field
or maybe that stink is a skunk
not many around here anymore
I used to hold my nose at the smell
today I wouldn't, just to relive it
near this road, cattails grew
I often picked some for a vase
you'll never see cattails here again
they're widening the turnpike
three lanes on each side
thousands of trees cut down
no more birds' nests
just traffic, ambulance and police sirens
black soot shrouds my house
it's leaching in at the windows
I don't open them now
I forgot to dig up the dahlia bulbs
guess there'll be no flowers this spring
it's getting darker
I hate when the clocks change
need lights to see the road
had the headlights fixed
they still don't work right
the car's old now—too many repairs
maybe it just needs to be junked
it's getting colder
the heater's not working
couldn't sleep again last night

it's so dark
I'm so tired
I want to go home
I want to sleep
I want to go back
there's no place to turn around.

Night Train

World War II—
soldiers, sailors, coast guardsmen, marines
a few civilians
grabbed every seat on the train
from Syracuse to New York.

After a ten-hour shift
in the emergency room I wanted sleep
and propped a discarded
Sears Roebuck catalogue
against the window to pillow my head.

A sailor in navy blues
plunked himself down beside me
saying he admired
my Cadet Nurse Corps uniform
especially the way it hugged my curves.

The whir of the train's wheels
rolled out a lullaby. My eyes closed
until I felt a hand against my leg.
Accidental?
I squeezed myself against the opposite armrest.

Sleep tugged my eyelids but that hand
wandered again to my leg.
No conductor, nearby passengers sprawled in slumber
others unwilling to change seats
forced me into the role of watchdog.

He never shut his eyes, never
closed his mouth. He talked
talked, talked about his passion—
sculpting women's legs
and for realism,
his need to touch them.

After eight hours of policing his errant hand
the train arrived at Grand Central Terminal.
He offered to carry my suitcase. I declined
and recommended for his next trip
a muzzle and handcuffs.

Retired Toe Shoes

They hang on a hook in the bedroom.
Each morning Aunt Anna's eyes linger
on those shoes—

applause at her stage entrance
rapt faces, the audience's hush
before bursts of applause
for her solos, her *pas de deux*
her curtsies slow, deep
the kiss of tossed roses
sweetness of rose bouquets
mingling with her musk-scented sweat
curtains open again and again
to clapping, shouts of *Bravo*
curtsy, curtsy, curtains close
insistent applause—curtains part once more
smiling, she greets admirers
hurrying toward the stage.

That smile returns
even as she places her crutches
against the bed.

Remembering My Friend Nane

Her hands transformed flour, water, butter, eggs
into *want more* crepes, croissants

gathered lilacs, lilies, roses from the garden
to dress each room

When she planted, weeded, her broad-brimmed hat
guarded against freckles on her fair skin

At her *stop the car* request
she bent to pick goldenrod, cattails, ferns

Nane imitated whistles of birds
cavorting at the feeder

On frosty nights, she tucked in her children
their blankets *up to the chin*

With her husband she played a favorite duet, Schubert's *Sonata for
    Piano*
Nane regaled friends with her rendition of *Ms. Otis Regrets*

A grin, and the elegant lady tossed
spitless spitballs at her husband

We shared the beauty of autumn leaves in the Berkshires
cold stone crabs, bayside, in Florida's Keys

heard rain pounding on our sheltering tin roof
above orange trees in Puerto Rico's mountains

felt a caress from the surf's foam
white-patterned lace on the brown sand

I can still see her Delft-blue eyes smiling, speaking welcome at her door
inside, a table laden with quiche, Brie, plum tarts, absinthe

I can still see her bringing honey cake, Swiss chocolate to us
giving coins to every street performer, every beggar

My friend Nane, so like Rachel
biblical *ayshes chayil*

who reaches out her hand to the needy...
words of kindness are on her tongue...

---

ayshes chayil: In Hebrew Bible from King Solomon's song of praise
to the ideal woman.

Sixties Reprise for Cousin Harry

He got stuck
on pot and hash
acid, speed
Zappa, Hendrix
couldn't climb out
from days
of long hair
torn jeans
easy sex on
the Chevy's back seat.

Got stuck
on *Mothers of Invention*
The Doors
nights in the Village
that slow sax
sneaking out windows.

Couldn't get out of the groove—
the record damaged
repeating, repeating
that same theme blasting
bustin' his head.

Got stuck
chugging beer
sick on the sidewalk
staggering home
mad, mad.

Friends all moved on
Movin' Up and Movin' On
suits, ties
BMWs, bank accounts
play a new tune.

**My Friend the Artist Gregorio Prestopino
Addresses His Portrait of His Mother,
*Standing Woman***

You stand beside apples, onions
carrots, waxed and corded provolone
sell your produce to eke out enough
nickels, dimes and quarters
to help pay rent.

Your coal black eyes dominate.
They follow me in the group of boys
kicking a can down the cobbled street
yelling, running, hitting a ball
with a broken stick from your onion crate.

You want to buy me Sunday shoes.
Your hands, red and numb with cold
weigh apples, sort potatoes, cut cheese.
I gave up penny caramels
—saved seven cents a week—
to buy you gloves for Christmas.

My Reflections on Henri Rousseau's *Sleeping Gypsy*

Hungry, the lion follows
the scent of flesh
finds a dark-skinned Gypsy woman
asleep on the white sand.

Some primeval notes
left in the heart of the lute
that lies at the Gypsy's side
stir strange feelings within the lion's breast.
This king, his domain diminished,
senses a kinship
with the Gypsy queen
whose fingers curl around a staff
once a royal scepter,
his regal white mane
seems counterpart to her white headdress
formerly a stately crown.
The red and gold
of her flowing robe
recall forest sunsets.

His kind is feared, gunned down for sport
imprisoned in zoos
her kind unwanted, driven out,
golden hoops and bangles gone.

Close to a glass-like sea
under a white sterile moon
he guards her
while she sleeps.

Valentine (Memo to My Husband)

Envelope me
but do not send.
Keep me
in your shirt pocket
close to your heart.

Workshop

Some poems
dodge
sidestep
play hide-and-seek.

Others insist—
arrive in the morning
when dreams dissolve
or at night, banishing sleep,
words invade
advance
charge
blitz the brain
flaunt themselves
strut
demand a flashlight and pencil.

I bring a skeleton to teammates
who help flesh it
straighten an arm, a leg
inflate the lungs
put an expression on its face

and it lives.

Imagining the Coming of *Moshiach*

A mist spreads over cities, countries, the world. The sun stands still. The time has come—peace on earth, revival of the dead. *Moshiach* prepares himself for the long awaited journey. He puts on his fringed garment, clothes, most comfortable shoes, smooths his sidelocks, adjusts his skullcap. Packs walnuts, raisins, two bottles of water. For his place of entry, he reviews the words of sages, rabbis, prophets, considers the holy cities—Jerusalem, Safed, Tiberias, Hebron. Folk legends designate, as *Moshiach's Path*, a space between two stone houses in a narrow alleyway in Safed. Impossible, he has eaten too many steaks and chips. He gives thought to Tiberias, but the enticement of its hot springs might delay his journey. Hebron, city of Israel's Matriarchs and Patriarchs? No. Its hilly terrain would be a deterrent. He decides on the most sacred city, Jerusalem. A private plane could fulfill the prophesy of flying in on a cloud or on the wings of an eagle. Too costly. Another option, riding a white donkey into Jerusalem. But where could he find a white donkey? Mr. M settles for a white Cadillac and telephones the rental company. Three hours and six phone calls later, no car. Everyone seems to have trouble finding his address. Next option—the subway. Rushing to the nearest station, he hustles down the steps, doesn't have the correct money. Although doing good deeds hastens the coming of *Moshiach*, no one helps. He ducks under the turnstile, races for the train to the echo of threats. Attempting to squeeze through the train's closing door, he is almost cut in two but regains his footing on the station floor. Subways are too slow, anyway. Hurrying upstairs to the street, he finds a Holiday Inn, grabs a shuttle bus to the airport. They ask the usual questions, "Did anyone give you something to deliver? Did you pack your own luggage? Take off your shoes." The metal detector's buzzer sounds. A security agent's hands move over his body—find a few Roman coins, two with Hebrew inscriptions, a Babylonian silver shekel. He dashes down a long corridor, up an escalator, down an escalator, gets to the gate as the plane taxies off the runway.

Mr. M sighs, "Too much trouble. And they're still not ready to receive me." Mr. M goes home, takes off his shoes, relaxes on the sofa, and reads from the Good Book. As for the mist over the world, religionists and scientists would debate it for centuries. As for the sun that stood still, they would call it the summer solstice.

Moshiach: Messiah. From Maimonides's *Book of Law,* folklore and writings by prophets and sages.

For My Daughter

Your sixtieth year—
I still feel your small hand
warm trusting in mine

Daughter

When you chose your home
six thousand miles away
the hole in my heart
would not heal

so much unsaid
so much more to say.

As a parting gift
I gave you
my favorite shawl
to keep you warm.

You soon put it aside
Not my color.

Time went by.
The shawl lay crumpled
under a pile of rummage
in the storage closet.

On my last visit, you said
you'd cleaned out the closet

gotten rid of stuff.
What about that shawl, I asked.
*I gave it to charity—
someone may need it.*

How Many Generations Can a Bunny Rabbit Live?

The story of the white terry cloth rabbit
began at my six-year-old daughter's recital
where, as Bunny, she danced her much practiced
demi plié, demi plié, demi pointe.

Bunny hibernated in a dresser drawer
until transported to Israel a generation later
where my daughter's daughter
breathed life into Bunny
while carrying her *Purim* basket filled
with lollipops, cookies and *hamantoshen*
to friends, family, the ill, and the elderly.

In the third generation, Bunny's slumber
was again interrupted.
Animated by my daughter's daughter's daughter
Bunny listened to the story of Queen Esther
hopped around in her classroom
and ate greens at a *Seudat Purim*,
before retiring for the next generation.

Purim: celebrates a victory over evil in ancient Persia
hamantoshen: three-cornered pastry filled with fruit or poppy seeds
Seudat Purim: obligatory festive meal

Shabbat in Jerusalem

Each Friday my daughter fulfills
centuries-old traditions—
cleaning, cooking, baking
putting coins aside for charity.
She gathers her family at her home—
husband, children, grandchildren, guests.
Dressed in holiday attire, they await
The Royal Bride, The Queen, *Shabbat.*

At sunset
rumbling trucks, screeching cars
come to rest
stores and restaurants, shuttered.
The *Sabbath* siren sounds
heralding the holy hour.
Candle lighting welcomes
beloved *Shabbat.*

Evening prayers
greetings of *Shabbat Shalom*
linger, mingle
with aromas of chicken soup
cholent, kugel, cake
the perfume of flowers.

Voices in song
drift through windows
blend with hymns
of love and praise to God
to *Shabbat, L'Cha Dodi*—Come My Dear One...
to Mother, *Ayshes Chayil*—Woman of Valor...
a blessing for each child
Sabbath candles, *challah,* wine.

Remember the Sabbath day
in your heart and soul
with joy and love and inner peace
Sabbath peace
stretches
through Saturday.

Hum of voices at morning prayers
families strolling home for midday meals
graced by guests as in Abraham's tent
chatter of children, shouts, laughter
playful breezes tease
clothing left on the line.

Released from weekday routines,
parents push baby carriages
swings fly on playgrounds
teenagers meet at youth groups
if boys flirt, girls pretend not to notice
car-cluttered streets transform into promenades
friends visit—coffee, cake, conversation
entire neighborhoods are kin.

For others, thoughts turn inward—
be a better person
help heal the world
come closer to God.
In homes and synagogues
discussions linger over Jewish law
a yearning for peace, beauty, mercy
the coming of *Moshiach*.

A leisurely meal
evening prayers
three stars in a darkened sky
the *Sabbath* Queen departs.

The family gathers at home
for the *havdalah* ceremony
marking the close of *Shabbat*
dividing it from weekdays.

A blessing, Father holds
a wine cup overflowing
signifying abundance and the essence
of *Shabbat* spilling into the new week.

A blessing, the spice container
is passed for everyone to smell
its aroma providing comfort
at *Shabbat's* departure.

A blessing, Father lifts the glowing *havdalah* candle
to symbolize separation of holiness from dailiness
dark from light, celebrating light and fire
God's creations for mankind's benefit.

A blessing, Father snuffs the *havdalah* candle
in a saucer with wine from the cup that *runneth over*
with song and greeting family and guests
welcome the new week, *shevuah tov*.

Your stones, O Jerusalem,
have seen civilizations rise and fall
and have come full circle
Pray for the Peace of Jerusalem
eternal *Sabbath* peace.

---

challah: braided bread for the Sabbath meal
cholent: meat, vegetable and bean stew
havdalah: separation
kugel: traditional pudding-like food of potatoes or noodles
Moshiach: Messiah
shevuah tov: a good week
Shabbat: *Sabbath*, from Friday's sundown to Saturday's sundown
Shabbat shalom: traditional greeting, *Sabbath* peace

Mothers and Daughters: Degrees of Love

Cool love asks,
Did you sleep well?
    No. I had a dreadful night.
You'll sleep better tomorrow.

Warm love asks,
Shall I rub your back,
make some hot soup
like when you were little?

    I prefer lemonade.
Soup is better.
    Not for me, I don't like it anymore.
    I want lemonade—ice cold.

Warm love brings lemonade
from the fridge
chilling her hands
then, drinks some.

Biopsy

When waiting for results
each nerve taut
negative and positive wrestle
in endless bouts—clutching, holding, throwing.

Finally, the phone call

that turns positive upside down
pins it to the mat
delivers at that moment
the sweetest word—

Negative,
The biopsy results are
Negative.

Absence of Roses

When he thought she had cancer
when he thought he might lose her
his voice became gentle
his touch loving
her habits endearing
red roses in his hand
smiles at piled-up books
and papers to-be-read.

When the crisis passed
again she tiptoed around
his cloudburst anger
chronic frown
thoughtless words
You're getting fat—
Why the long face?
You can't even take a joke,
hurtful words
Get rid of those piles of papers
those magazines, those beat-up books
or I'm throwing them out!

Ritual

Your distracted peck
smacks more of husbandly duty
than of Cupid's bow

Cataract Surgery

I picked up your jacket.
In the pocket
lay a report,
"HIV positive."

After fifty years
of marriage
the opaque film
removed

I see you clearly.

Pieris Rapae, the Cabbage Moth

I hate the white moth with black spots
that descends upon the cabbage

lays its eggs on the leaf—
green worms hatch

feed on tender new leaves
penetrate the cabbage, eat rapaciously

leave holes
black droppings.

Still, the cabbage grows large and green—
damaged inside.

Plans Upended: A Tale Told by My Greek Mythology Professor

He bribed the Ferryman in advance
to row his soul to the Elysian Fields.

Charon took a wrong turn.

Bump and Butt of Passing Years

Can't drink coffee
can't eat candy

can't drink liquor
can't eat spices

pink pills, appetizer
white pills, dessert

sex, a memory
coming in dreams

hate the cold
can't take the sun

New Jersey too damp
Arizona too dry

clothes don't fit
too tired to shop

jowls sag
breasts hang

nose bigger
eyes smaller

long luxurious hair
grows in the nose

synapses lazy
response time down

sleepy all day
awake all night

I'll write a poem
can't find my glasses

Primavera Everlasting

February in New Jersey, 2012
   violets, roses
      snapdragons, azaleas
 bloom
    In halcyon days
      daffodils and irises
flourish

Some call
   seventy degrees in winter
     global warming
Others believe
   prayers
       performance of good deeds
may abolish winter
bring eternal spring—

color returns
   to white hair
wrinkles
   unwrinkle
 ninety-year olds
 run
   marathons
burn
   canes for firewood
revel
   in the pleasures of the bed

But I think that Nature
went carousing with Dionysus

May they stay
    in
eb   ri
  a
  ted

On Reaching a 90th Birthday

An overly ripe peach
with brown spots and withered
decay sets in

Old Age Home

Now a euphemism—"Continuing Care"
still a holding pen
until the Judge's final sentence

Stars' Promise

Pieces of day
survive in the night sky
bright holes in the dark

Beverly Mach Geller is a graduate of Syracuse University School of Nursing. After careers in nursing and interior design, she majored in English, earning a BA from Rutgers University and an MA from The College of NJ. The author of seven books for children including a book of children's poetry *My Family and Me,* Geller received the Jane McHugh Memorial Senior Award for one of her poems. Her poetry for adults and children has been published in literary journals and anthologies including *Delaware Valley Poets, NJ Poetry Society, US1 Worksheets, U.S.1 Summer Fiction Edition, Kelsey Review, Poem Train* and *Jewish Women's Literary Annual.* Her poem "Shabbat in Jerusalem" is featured on derondareview.org. Her chapbook, *Daily Bread,* was published in 2013.